SELECTED POEMS OF

Salvador Espriu

Also by Salvador Espriu

POETRY

Cementiri deSinera (Cemetery of Sinera)
Cançons d'Ariadna (Songs of Ariadna)
Les hores (The Hours)
Mrs. Death
El caminant i el mur (The Walker and the Wall)
Final del laberint (End of the Labyrinth)
La pell de brau (The Bull's Skin)
Llibre de Sinera (Book of Sinera)
Setmana Santa (Holy Week)

PROSE

El Doctor Rip (Doctor Rip)
Laia (Laia)
Aspectes (Aspects)
Ariadna al laberint grotesc (Ariadne in the Grotesque Labyrinth)
Miratge a Citerea (Mirage at Citerea)
Letizia (Letitia)
Fedra (Phaedra)
Petites proses blanques (Small White Texts)
La pluja (The Rain)
Les roques i el mar, el blau (The Rocks and the Sea, the Blue)

DRAMA

Primera història d'Esther (First Story of Esther)
Antígona (Antigone)

Also by the translator, Magda Bogin

The Women Troubadours

Translations
House of the Spirits by Isabel Allende
El Angel's Last Conquest by Elvira Orphée
Selected Poems of Rosario Castellanos

SELECTED
POEMS OF
Salvador Espriu

SELECTED AND TRANSLATED

WITH A PREFACE BY

MAGDA BOGIN

AND AN INTRODUCTION BY

FRANCESC VALLVERDÚ

W · W · NORTON & COMPANY

NEW YORK   LONDON

Published simultaneously in Canada by Penguin Books Canada Ltd., 2801 John
Street, Markham, Ontario L3R 1B4.
Printed in the United States of America.

The text of this book is composed in Bembo.
Composition and manufacturing by The Maple-Vail Book Manufacturing Group.
Book design by Margaret M. Wagner.

First Edition

Library of Congress Cataloging in Publication Data

Espriu, Salvador.
  Selected poems of Salvador Espriu.

  Translation of selected poems in Poesia, which
is v. 1 of Obres completes.
  I. Bogin, Magda.   II. Title.
PC3941.E84A23   1988   849'.9152   88–5194

ISBN 0-393-02608-6

W. W. Norton & Company, Inc., 500 Fifth Avenue, New York, N.Y. 10110

W. W. Norton & Company Ltd., 37 Great Russell Street, London WC1B 3NU

1 2 3 4 5 6 7 8 9 0

Magda Bogin wishes to acknowledge the generous support of the National Endowment of the Arts and the Columbia Translation Center, and expresses her thanks to the Writer's Room in New York City, where final work on this book was completed.

Earlier versions of the following poems appeared in *The American Poetry Review:*
"Parca," "Here the voyage ends," "Book of the Dead," "Song of Triumphant Night," "Don't you hear the sound the hoe makes," "Old Brueghel Told It Thus," "Remember us," and "Song of Evening's Arriving."

The following poems appeared in *Boulevard:*
"Parca" and "Wind."

For my sister,

Nina Bogin

Contents

Contents

I I

I I I

I V

Contents

Translator's Preface

> I have given my whole life to words,
> chewed this dog-hunger into a long meal.
> Have mercy, sentry, on these bones,
> for I arrive without a scrap of flesh!

Salvador Espriu was not yet forty when he wrote these lines, the opening of "Offering to Cerberus," one of the most haunting poems in *Les hores/The Hours*. The same collection, his third, also contains the poem "Prometheus":

> I brought them glass and blaze of words,
> bright names spoken by old lips of fire . . .
> . . . .
> With your beak you shall tear eternal paths
> to the blood I offer as the price of this gift.

Readers who know the exuberance and grandeur of Neruda or the patterned lyricism of García Lorca may be taken aback by Espriu's sober, deeply philosophical poems, by his precocious embrace of death. His line is taut, his words few, his cadence measured, almost religiously so. The pleasure he takes in language is painterly, but not robust; musical, but with its grave repetitions, more like Gregorian chant than modern song. His syllables glow, not with the energy of his contemporaries and fellow Catalans Tàpies and Miró, but with the darker tones of Goya or El Greco: "I plunged my hands," he writes, again in *The Hours,* "into the mysterious gold of my beloved Catalan."

Certainly temperament accounts in part for the cryptic condensation, the metaphysical density, of Espriu's poetry. But something more is required to explain a lifetime dedicated to writing what may strike some readers as a series of epitaphs for his own grave. That *more* is history, and the watershed event of Espriu's life and the life of his country in this century: the Civil War that cleft Spain in two beginning in July of 1936.

Spain, the land Espriu would call "this bull's skin / thick with blood," was already sixteen years into the nightmare of the Franco years when *The Hours* appeared in 1952, and Espriu had long since been writing the slow, tensile, musical poems that set him utterly apart from the other poets of his generation. Already, as poems like "Prometheus" and "Offering to Cerberus" amply show, his work was charged with a sense of mission that can only be fully grasped by understanding the accumulated losses and passionate attachments to which he felt himself heir.

"You don't know what the years '39, '40, '41, '42, '43, '45, '46, '47, '48, '49, '50 and a good part of the following decade were," Espriu told an interviewer in 1968, making explicit the burden his poetry conveys in other ways: not time's passage but its weight in the aftermath of the war and Franco's triumph:

> I alone and the hours,
> and my dead moving off
> one by one down long
> rows of silence.

Rarely has history embedded itself so deeply, or so articulately, in a single life. Twenty-five at the end of the war and already a published novelist, Espriu turned to poetry almost as a monk to prayer, embarking on the "internal exile," as the critic Maria Aurelia Campany calls it, that would become almost fifty years of continuous poetic labor.

His master? Memory, the protean force that pressed Espriu's
poetic line to mythic spareness and that pressed him forward,
in book after book, along one of the twentieth century's lone-
liest and most extraordinary poetic journeys.

> I lose myself and am alone, with no message,
> beyond song, among the forgotten,
> those who fell in fear, merely a dark dream
> of one who stepped from the palaces of light.

Words weigh here, and with good reason. If memory lives
in language, words are the living icons that distill as genes do
the collective life of a whole people. Dictators know this, and
when a language is banned, as was Catalan—the beautiful, stark,
ancient language of Northern Spain that was Espriu's mother
tongue—after Franco triumphed, each forbidden word becomes
an act of preservation and defiance; an act, literally, of imagi-
nation, of breathing life—the image—back into the word.

To have a language is to have a past, but also a future. And
to keep the language was to keep the faith, even when faith
itself, except perhaps in some sort of latter-day negative capa-
bility, was no longer possible:

> You know too well that nothing lies beyond, except
> the still, cold, solitary, dark
> light, stairs and wells of light, where words
> flicker and are lost, riders on the back of silence.

To use a forbidden language to evoke not only the lost past
or hoped-for future but the very impossibility of language, is
perhaps the ultimate act of defiance. Yet it is precisely this exis-

tential task—this insistence on the word as both signified and signifier while simultaneously questioning the capacity of language (*any* language) to signify at all—that Espriu took upon himself almost as a form of expiation, as if he could somehow, by working and reworking the same small lexicon, wrest from fate the "few bright, fragile / words of song" that would redeem what he called "our time already dead":

> We shall give each thing a final name
> as old memory shapes an almost new creation.

If Espriu is a mystic—his work is saturated with allusions to the monuments of Greek, Christian, Jewish, and Islamic mysticism—this is not the ecstatic vision of San Juan de la Cruz and Saint Teresa but the deep inwardness of Raimon Llull, the thirteenth-century Catalan mystic who renounced the world, or the grim, divided vision of Ausias March, the fourteenth-century poet whose brooding *Cants de mort* ("Songs of Death") remain the towering achievement of Catalan verse. It is to this quintessentially Catalan tradition that Espriu's poetry, with its "contained religiosity" (as the critics Josep Castellet and Joaquim Mola call it), belongs; and it was with this tradition, certainly, that Espriu himself identified in describing all his poems as a single lifelong meditation on the theme of death.

The poet's lifetime of mourning begins in the tiny cemetery of Arenys (anagrammatically transformed to Sinera), the Mediterranean village up the coast from Barcelona where Espriu spent much of his childhood and where he is buried. The opening

poem of *Cementiri de Sinera / Cemetery of Sinera,* his first pub-
lished collection, stakes out the mythical terrain—the *petita patria*
or "little nation"—that will become the ground on which he
will build his entire poetics.

The ancestral past, a graveyard but also a small world: Cata-
lonia, the necessary ground on which Espriu's redeeming vision
of the future—impossible, desired—will rise.

> What a little nation
> rings the graveyard!
> This sea, Sinera,
> hills of pines and vines,
> dusty riverbeds. There is nothing
> I love more, except the roving
> shadow of a cloud.
> The slow memory of days
> forever gone.

Sinera; sea; hills; vines; memory; words that in Espriu's cos-
mos acquire the unequivocal resonance of myth:

> House, hill, ship,
> deep breath of water,
> clear rose. With words
> always new I clothe
> the newborn evening.

Espriu, not the Catalan language (as rich as any Romance
tongue), has imposed this narrow lexicon, in which the sim-
plest words are burnished to an elemental, almost sacral, power:
the words of landscape, the elements, death itself.

Urban life is conspicuously absent from these poems, even though Espriu spent his life in Barcelona, and there are few identifiable men and women; Espriu's world is the ancient one of myth and archetype. The presences too are mythic: the rag-man, the beggar, the leper; Prometheus, Tiresias, Salom, the name Espriu gave himself.

And Spain, which Espriu (in a stroke that may at first seem strange in view of his essentially Christian sensibility) calls Sepharad, its Hebrew name. But to what more fitting tradition could Espriu turn when faced with the terrible exodus of his own time, which saw more than a million Spaniards flee Fascism for exile abroad, than to that of the Spanish Jews, the Sephardim expelled from Spain in 1492? Again and again in *La pell de brau / The Bull's Skin,* his seventh and most popular book, the poet invokes that lost, wounded, irretrievable Spain as he speaks of a generation "still scattered / in the wind and wandering / of the Golah," the Hebrew word for the diaspora.

Espriu, who hated what he called "vanity's obscene expansion," gave few interviews, but when he agreed to talk he was always interesting. "You have before you a man who can claim to be one hundred and sixty-eight years old," he told Santos Hernández, the Spanish translator of *The Bull's Skin.* "What he was telling me," Hernández writes in his introduction to that volume, "was that . . . through generations of conversation, he had heard eyewitness accounts of Napoleon's invasion of Arenys."

It is that ancient voice—the voice of the blind man, of the seer Tiresias and the redeemer Prometheus, the voice of Salom and Sepharad—that speaks, through the Catalan voice of Salvador Espriu, "the few bright words" of universal meaning that make the journey worth it.

THE SHAPE OF THIS BOOK

To reduce Espriu's nine major books of poems to a representative selection in English has been no mean task. In a poet of Espriu's caliber, who not only worked each poem until it shone like a small stone but who revised even his published work throughout his life, the only reasonable approach was to do rough drafts of all four hundred or so poems—to give them all an equal chance, so to speak, at inclusion. My intent was not to produce a scholarly selection, proportionately reflecting each of the poet's many voices, but rather to create a book of poems that worked in English: a book with a life of its own, analogous (I like to think) to the inner life that animates each of the original nine books.

Some of Espriu's poems are famous in Spain; some of these have been set to music and have a political resonance—both because of their overt content and because of the contexts in which they have been sung—that is not immediately transferable to English. Some have been widely anthologized, both in Catalan and in Spanish translation. Yet those whose appeal is most immediate in Spain were not always those that worked best in my first round of drafts. The final selection was made after working "up" from the first drafts to second versions. I kept those poems that began to live in English, and left the rest, regrettably, behind.

The result is as personal a choice as any selection is bound to be. The book begins with poems from Espriu's earliest work, moves through the middle books with some of the later poems included to foreshadow his deepening vision, to a mixture of his late and early poems, ending with the final poem of *Cemetery of Sinera*. The five selections from *Cançons d' Ariadna / Songs of Ariadna,* the one "dissonant" book in Espriu's oeuvre, in which he exercised his wit and mastery of form (often with the mad-cap rhymes so reminiscent of the troubadours) have been dis-tributed throughout the collection in analogy to that book's role for the poet: as a counterweight, written over the course of many years, to the graver voice that dominates his work.

There is also a progression, as in the poetry itself, from the poem as canticle—one of Espriu's recurring words—to what in his later poems he called the "naked rock of song," a progres-sion mirrored thematically by the poet's move from the ceme-tery of Sinera through the long dispersal of the Golah and Sepharad, back to a Sinera reclaimed and made larger by the journey.

I like to think that Espriu, who died before this work could be completed, would have accepted the idea of this "book of books," which closes the circle of his life and work to end with his beginning.

A NOTE ON THE TRANSLATION

Certain little known affinities between Catalan and English assist the translator. Both languages are rich in monosyllables, with all the rhymic and aural possibilities that fact implies: a wealth of spondees, heady enjambments, clusters of consonants. This makes Catalan far more compatible with English than Spanish or Italian. The poetry of both languages relies for its music on the subtleties of assonance and internal rhyme. And Catalan, which suffered a three-centuries' decline between the late Renaissance and the dawn of the Industrial Age, has a freshness of both image and diction that allows for certain comparisons to the spring of American English, whose arrival as a literary language is comparably late.

Still, no translation, no matter how "good," or how conscientious, is ever definitive; it is a reading, no more. And not even a collective one. Being democratically inclined and fortunate enough to have a publisher who agreed, I have been able to include the original Catalan on facing pages. Astute readers of this book will see the loss from left to right—the order of thought sacrificed to the rigid word order of English, syllable counts slightly awry, rhymes (particularly in the poems from *Songs of Ariadna*) hinted at instead of caught. Translation is a writer's gamble, a rope thrown to another shore. If there is any tug at all, I will be satisfied.

My gratitude to Nina Bogin, who read this, as she reads all manuscripts, with exquisite care; to Allen Mandelbaum, whose exigence remains a model; to Jane Cooper, for her unerring ear; to David Curzon, for precision mathematical and poetic; to Rodolfo Cardona, for attention beyond the call of duty; to Mary Ann Newman, peerless reader and Catalanista without peer; to Kathleen Anderson, who first took this project on at Norton; to Jill Bialosky, who gave it continued life; and to Francesc Vallverdú of Edicions 62 in Barcelona, whose own introduction follows.

MAGDA BOGIN
New York

Introduction

In 1964, when I was a young poet of twenty-eight, I had the good fortune of meeting Salvador Espriu, by then a famous writer with most of his published work behind him. I had admired him ever since I was a teen-ager, when his early work had made an indelible impression on me. From then until Espriu fell gravely ill at the end of 1984, my relationship with him was uninterrupted, and despite the difference in our ages, we became great friends.

In a world in which personal relations are becoming ever colder and more superficial, Espriu was a survival from another age. He was a wonderful conversationalist, and liked to hear about the "outside world" from which by then he had virtually withdrawn, having isolated himself within his family—he lived with a brother and sister-in-law—and in his job as legal counsel to a medical insurance company.

To some degree, of course, this image of Espriu as a social isolate is misleading; the fact that in his final twenty years he had little or no social life should not imply that he was uninterested in the doings of the street. First of all, thanks to the handful of friends who continued to visit him and to his voracious reading, Espriu was always well informed about the latest developments in literary and intellectual life. I was continually amazed by his knowledge of contemporary writers (he read both English and French with ease). In another realm, Espriu was always deeply affected by the political vicissitudes of Catalonia and Spain under Franco. Along with other Catalan and Spanish intellectuals, he signed innumerable statements of protest, ranging from demands for the freedom to speak and write in Catalan to denunciations of brutality and torture at the hands of the Falangist police. His isolation, then, should be viewed not as evidence of any lack of solidarity, but rather as an act in accord with his high conception of literature.

Espriu's desire for perfection led him constantly to revise his poems and stories, an activity he did not relinquish until the eve of his death. He firmly believed that a writer is unworthy of the name unless he or she takes full responsibility for every text, down to the last comma, and we often spent hours discussing words or expressions about which he was unsure. The simple, unadorned surface of his poems hides a poet of great sensitivity and vast humanistic culture, who strives to articulate the most exact expression and most potent symbols with the fewest possible words. One could say, in fact, that Espriu is one of the few Hispanic poets who was true to the words of the great theorist of the Baroque, Baltasar Gracián: *lo bueno, si breve, dos veces bueno* ("the good, when brief, is twice as good").

Of all the writers I have known, and I have known many, I have met none with a personality as firm, as fascinating, and as inextricably linked to his art as Salvador Espriu. Those lucky enough to have known him will always recall his great generosity toward his friends—for surely to spend one's time talking and listening is one of the clearest signs of generosity—his acute mind as a reader, and his enormous cordiality, as well as a sense of humor that could take those who didn't know him by surprise.

The present anthology is not only a fine overall introduction to the poetry of Salvador Espriu (1913–85), but also a careful selection in which Espriu's main poetic voices are each given their due. But before turning to the individual poems, we need to look at the full range of his writing, and at the historical and intellectual circumstances that led Espriu to abandon fiction for theater and poetry.

It is important to keep in mind that in 1931, when Espriu was a young writer of eighteen, the Second Republic was proclaimed in Spain, and that Catalonia—a country with its own language and culture, as well as a strong national personality—was immediately granted autonomy for the first time since its annexation by the Spanish crown in 1714.

At long last, Catalonian writers enjoyed a measure of public recognition. Hundreds of books were published in Catalan each year, and there were numerous newspapers and magazines as well. Throughout this period of literary and cultural ferment (whose most notable development was the founding of the bilingual Autonomous University of Catalonia) the young Espriu was an interested but critical voice. More inclined temperamentally toward scepticism, and more able than some of his contemporaries to detect the weaknesses of Catalan society, he seems to have foreseen the Civil War (1936–39) that would be the fatal outcome of those years.

Still, at this point, there was nothing to suggest that the precocious young writer, who had published his first book at seventeen, would soon be a great poet. Espriu was busy establishing himself as a spare, incisive narrator. His books, which oscillated between lyricism and irony, were increasingly well received by both critics and readers, and his storytelling talent seemed naturally to lead to prose. *El doctor Rip* (1931), *Laia* (1932), *Aspectes* (1934), *Ariadna al laberint grotesc* (1935), *Miratge a Citerea* (1935), and *Letizia* (1936), all novels and short stories, attest not only to his feverish activity, but also to the existence of a public interested in the books of this extraordinarily young writer.

These facts have led a number of critics to conclude, perhaps precipitously, that Espriu's origin as a poet is to be found in an external event: the Civil War.

Indeed, the Civil War and its consequences took a deep toll on him; Espriu essentially fell silent after Franco's victory, when the Catalan language was singled out for punishment. Books, newspapers, and magazines in Catalan were banned, schools were required to teach only in Spanish, and Catalan, having ceased to be the official language of Catalunya, could not be spoken in public. Writers were the most direct victims of the repression. Is this why Espriu turned to poetry after 1939?

Certainly, the Civil War was a traumatic experience for him, not so much because of any personal tribulations, which were few (since he was a lawyer, he did his military service in the offices of the Military Courts and suffered no reprisals with the fall of the Republic), but because of what he witnessed: the revolutionary upheavals in Barcelona, with the resulting persecution and assassination of innocent people, the devastating bombardments of the city, and the death of friends and family, among them that of his close friend Bartomeu Rosselló-Pòrcel, who died of tuberculosis in 1938.

Clearly, the Espriu of 1939 was himself—and yet he was another. But changes in personality do not occur overnight. The first thing he wrote after Franco's triumph was a play: *Antigone,* a new vision of the myth of war between brothers, directly traceable to his own experience of civil war. This work, which was pacifist and reconciliatory in nature, would not be published until 1955, nine years after Franco's censors had authorized the publication of books in Catalan.

And the first poems Espriu composed after the war were satires and songs linked to the stories in *Aspects* and *Ariadna in the*

Grotesque Labyrinth: these are the poems from *Les cançons d'Ariadna / Songs of Ariadna,* which Espriu considered his first book despite the fact that he wrote it over many years. The inclusion of only five of them here is entirely in keeping with the poet's own view of the place of this book in his whole oeuvre.

Still, there can be no doubt that the deep transformation that would make Espriu one of the great European lyric poets of the twentieth century was already underway. *Cementiri de Sinera / Cemetery of Sinera* (1946), written between 1944 and 1945, is the first example of his work in that new vein and the first book of poetry he published. "Sinera" is a made-up name derived from reversing the letters of Arenys—the fishing village some fifteen miles up the coast from Barcelona, where Espriu spent most of his childhood and where both his parents had been born. Sinera, then, symbolizes the poet's roots, and its cemetery is the place where his loved ones have been laid to rest: parents, relatives, friends. This poetry is elegiac but not nostalgic, if by nostalgia we mean the longing for better times. It is also the record of the "tiny nation" that has been devastated by suffering and death: the *petita patria* of the poem that opens both *Cemetery of Sinera* and this anthology. Hardly surprising then, that Espriu—who considered poetry "a small help in living an upright life and perhaps in dying a good death"—reveals himself in this small masterpiece in all his greatness and singularity.

It would be followed by *Les hores / The Hours* (1952), part of which was linked thematically to his earlier narrative. *The Hours* should be placed in the same vein as *Cemetery;* here too the elegiac impulse is pervasive. Yet only two of the three sections, each dedicated to a loved one who has died, are "authentic": the first, which is inscribed to the memory of Bartomeu Rosselló-

Pòrcel, the poet's close friend; and the second, which is dedicated to Espriu's mother. The third is in memory of the poet's *alter ego,* Salom, who is said to have died on July 18, 1936, the day the Spanish Civil War began. Obviously this third section (represented in this collection by the beautiful poems "Prometheus," "Omnis fortasse moriar," and "Offering to Cerberus") does not have the same elegiac tone; the lyricism of these poems, which is not without a certain sarcasm, stems from the poet's frustration and the hopes and illusions of his youth.

The reflection that began with the third part of *The Hours* continues in the book that followed it, *Mrs. Death,* titled in English, the universal tongue *par excellence,* as if wishing to avoid the "sentimental" explicitness of its Catalan equivalent. While it is perhaps less unified a book than *Cemetery* or than the individual parts of *The Hours,* the Catalan critic Josep Castellet, the most important interpreter of Espriu's poetry, has nonetheless identified two distinct voices in this book. The first, to which the poems "Song of Tiresias" and "Marriage" belong, contains satirical poems on archetypes and situations from daily life. "Diptych of the Living," also included in the present collection, serves as a stepping stone to the next part, in which the theme of death is clearly a part of life. The four other poems from *Mrs. Death* included here represent other themes to which Espriu returned again and again: death as silence, the stairs that lead to nothingness, and childhood memory as a refuge from present evil.

The *Walker and the Wall* is another of Espriu's subdivided books. In the first part, subtitled "The Shadows, the River, the Lost Dream" (from which Magda Bogin has drawn three short poems), memory appears as a form of salvation in the face of death, and the grief of a people is sufficient reason for the poet's word. The second, "Songs of the Wheel of Time," contains twelve gently elegiac poems (four of which appear in this collection) representing the different positions of the sun throughout the day, or the twelve signs of the Zodiac. The third part, "The Minotaur and Theseus," contains several of the most important compositions from Espriu's later work, six of which are included here. "Ish, Isha, Eli, Elis" sets forth the relationship between man and God in tones reminiscent of the Book of Job and concludes on a provocative, almost blasphemous note, while "Felt in the Manner of Salvador Espriu" restates the poet's solitude and sense of impotence.

This last poem is linked to the first poem of *End of the Labyrinth,* by far the most cryptic of Espriu's books. According to Castellet, several new themes make their appearance here, including the mystical journey, with its ascent to the "mountain." While Espriu also makes use of images and symbols that had not appeared before in his poems—the labyrinth, the shepherd, the hunter, the four elements, "white words"—interpretation remains difficult. Only the two quotations that serve as epigraphs, one from Meister Eckhart and the other from Nicholas of Cusa, provide a clue, suggesting "negative theology" (or the view that all that can be known of God is that which is not known) as the structural underpinning of this book, which marks the close of another chapter in Espriu's creative life.

By the late 1950s, changes began to occur on the Spanish political landscape. After a period of outright persecution of all things Catalan, the Franco regime moved toward more attenuated forms of repression, so that there was now a small degree of tolerance for Catalan culture. It was then that Espriu felt himself "called" to a "prophetic mission" and that he wrote *La pell de brau / The Bull's Skin* (1960), whose title refers to the shape of the Iberian peninsula on the map. The book was an immediate success, and was quickly translated into Spanish, French, and Portuguese. Castellet attributes the widespread popularity of several of these poems to the fact that for once Espriu was writing "objective poetry in which each word can be understood . . . and is complete unto itself . . . there are not the usual obsessions and ambiguities we have come to expect from the poet." Of course, Castellet continues, "This kind of poetry . . . was that least characteristic of Espriu."

Espriu himself was surprised by the book's success, particularly because *The Bull's Skin* was generally presented as "political poetry," which it was not. True, its roots lay in a meditation on the adventures and misadventures of the Catalan people, and more broadly, of Spain and Portugal (at the time both under dictatorial regimes); Espriu's attitude, however, was not so much political as it was "prophetic" in the Hebraic tradition.

This moral stance recurs in his next book, *El llibre de Sinera / The Book of Sinera* (1963), where the poet, as if to escape the abusive interpretations critics had given to *The Bull's Skin,* trained his gaze on Catalan reality. But Sinera here becomes far more than the mythification of Arenys, Espriu's ancestral town, and comes to represent all Catalonia, the poet's national community, seen with a very personal vision: there is a constant tension between the poet's subjectivity and the historical process of his "tiny nation." Not by chance is it in this book that for the first time we find a revealing acrostic (impossible to translate into English): in Catalan, the first letters of the last four lines of the final poem ("But in thirst the pine takes root") spell the word *mort,* death, which this time appears as definitive and irremediable, or, in Castellet's view, as the "culmination of a life and a work."

This collection contains four compositions from the carefully metered *Holy Week,* the last great poetic work Espriu wrote. Here, in poems whose form he hoped would closely mirror the ideas or feelings he expressed, Espriu once again expresses his fatalistic view of human nature. But he also upholds the grandeur of the individual who, tragically aware of his own wretchedness, transcends it.

FRANCESC VALLVERDÚ
Barcelona
Translated from the Catalan by Magda Bogin

I

Quina petita pàtria
encercla el cementiri!
Aquesta mar, Sinera,
turons de pins i vinya,
pols de rials. No estimo
res més, excepte l'ombra
viatgera d'un núvol.
El lent record dels dies
que són passats per sempre.

What a little nation
rings the graveyard!
This sea, Sinera,
hills of pines and vines,
dusty riverbeds. There is nothing
I love more, except the roving
shadow of a cloud.
The slow memory of days
forever gone.

A la vora del mar. Tenia
una casa, el meu somni,
a la vora del mar.

Alta proa. Per lliures
camins d'aigua, l'esvelta
barca que jo manava.

Els ulls sabien
tot el repòs i l'ordre
d'una petita pàtria.

Com necessito
contar-te la basarda
que fa la pluja als vidres!
Avui cau nit de fosca
damunt la meva casa.

Les roques negres
m'atrauen a naufragi.
Captiu del càntic,
el meu esforç inútil,
qui pot guiar-me a l'alba?

Ran de la mar tenia
una casa, un lent somni.

Beside the sea. I had
a house, my dream,
beside the sea.

High prow. I sailed
my agile skiff
along free waterways.

My eyes knew
all the peace and order
of a little land.

How I need to tell you
what dread the rain awakens
on the windowpanes!
Today dark night falls
on my house.

Black rocks
draw me to shipwreck.
Captive of canticle,
my effort vain,
who will lead me to the dawn?

At the sea's edge I had
a house, a slow dream.

Pels portals de Sinera
passo captant engrunes
de vells records. Ressona
als carrers en silenci
el feble prec inútil.
Cap caritat no em llesca
el pa que jo menjava,
el temps perdut. M'esperen
tan sols, per fer-me almoina,
fidels xiprers verdíssims.

I knock at Sinera's
doors, begging crumbs
of ancient memories. My frail
useless prayer echoes
in the silent streets.
No charity cuts the
bread I used to eat,
the lost time. The only
almsgivers here are
cypresses, faithful and bolt-green.

Parca

Jo, només, i les hores,
i els meus morts que s'allunyen
a poc a poc per llargues
rengleres de silenci.

Temo al mirall un rostre
excessiu i sobtades
nits amb veus, la profunda
certitud de les coses.

Tot és en va. Vells ecos
de respostes buidaven
de sentit la ferida
que sóc, tan sols un home.

On, per què? No sabria
dir-m'ho mai, però sento
com aquells dits em filen,
enllà de mars, d'escuma
d'estranys somnis, un únic
camí sense fugida.

Parca

I alone and the hours,
and my dead moving off
step by step down long
rows of silence.

I'm afraid of an extra face
in the mirror and sudden
nights with voices, the deep
certainty of things.

Everything is in vain. Old
echoes of answers drain
the meaning from the wound
I am, only a man.

Where? Why? I don't know
how to put it, but I feel
those fingers weaving me,
beyond seas, from the foam
of strange dreams, a single
path without escape.

Matrimoni

Tanca el ponent a fora,
tot l'estiu, la parada
fatiga de suburbi,
geranis i falcies.

Tens ordenada i neta
i a punt la nostra casa
oi que sí? De seguida
començarem a dir-nos,
potser, velles paraules.

Te'n riuràs, però sento
dintre, de sobte, rares
veus de Déu i manubris,
set de gos i missatge
de lents records que es perden
part enllà d'un pont fràgil.
I tu portes la tassa
de malalt i en silenci
t'asseus, mentre ens condemnen
els anys, els morts, l'enorme
balcó roent del vespre.

Marriage

All summer long sunset
stops outside, the still
fatigue of the slums,
geraniums and swifts.

You keep our house
neat as a pin and clean,
don't you? Soon,
perhaps, we'll speak to each other
with old words.

You may laugh, but I feel
within me, suddenly, strange
voices of God and handles,
dog's thirst and message
of slow memories that disappear
across a fragile bridge.
You bring the sick man's
cup and sit in silence while
the years, the dead, the great
fiery balcony of dusk
condemn us.

Escala

M'han vençut en la lluita
d'un dia breu. I a l'altre,
tot ja serà tenebra.

On les fonts pures, l'alba
d'un somni fosc? Pregunto,
descendint per l'escala
del meu temps, al silenci
que en mi esdevenia.

No se m'atansen llavis
a dir-me cap resposta.
Sols puc recordar passos
i l'extingit domini
dels meus morts, i perdudes
cançons, i la tristesa
de després, quan em feien
aquest mal inguarible.

Stairs

They conquered me in the struggle
of one brief day. By tomorrow
all will be shadow.

Where is the pure source, the dawn
of a dark dream? Descending
the staircase of my time,
I ask the silence
growing inside me.

No lips approach
to answer me.
All I can recall are footsteps
and the vanished kingdom
of my dead, and lost
songs, and the sadness
that came next, when they gave me
this incurable grief.

El jardí dels cinc arbres

Després, quan ja m'havia
fet molt de mal i quasi
sols podia somriure,
vaig triar les paraules
més senzilles, per dir-me
com passà un momentani
or de sol damunt l'heura
del jardí dels cinc arbres.
Groc brevíssim, de posta,
a l'hivern, mentre queien
els últims dits de l'aigua
serpentina, d'alts núvols,
i el temps estrany m'entrava
en presons de silenci.

The Garden of Five Trees

Later, when I was already
in great pain and almost all
I could do was smile,
I chose the simplest
words to tell myself
how the sun's momentary
gold had crossed the ivy
of the garden of five trees.
Fleeting yellow, of sunset,
in winter, while the winding
water's final fingers
fell from the high clouds
and the strange time entered me
in jails of silence.

En la teva mort

Fustes sonores, cròtals,
secrets tam-tams de selva
avisen com augmentes
en dolor, impossible
de retornar-te a límits
on pot encara dir-se,
singular, la pregària.
Madur d'empreses, ídol
a temples momentanis,
nostre record, t'allunyes
avui per glaços, càntic
tot anul·lat en pluja.

On Your Death

Wood blocks, rattles,
secret forest tam–tams
tell your rising
pain, impossible
to lead you back now to limits where
this singular prayer
can still be said.
Ripe with plans, idol
of fleeting shrines,
our memory, you disappear
today in ice, canticle
wiped clean by rain.

Arbre

Jo et vaig somniar majestat invisible
que plana per la faç de cada cosa.
Arrelat en dolor de la cendra,
un home només, et portava, sepulcre,
pare mort, dintre meu, en silenci,
i et cridava amb paraules de vent
d'antics mil·lenaris, que encenen la ira.
No has respost mai al clam i em deixaves
en temença de nit, foc secret, alta flama,
arbre Déu en la nit.

Tree

I dreamt you invisible majesty
hovering above the face of all things.
Rooted in the pain of ash,
mere man, I bore you, sepulchre,
dead father, silently, within,
called out to you the windswept words
of lost millennia, words that kindle rage.
You never answered me. You left me
fearing night, hidden fire, leaping flame,
tree God in the night.

El curs de la vida

Enllà del camí, m'he dit
paraules d'un vell dolor,
allunyada de claror,
per sempre, la meva nit.
Als llavis no torna el crit
en lent càntic, car enlloc
no defugiria el toc,
cor endins, del temps perdut.
I esdevé, somni romput,
poca cendra de molt foc.

The Course of Life

Beyond the road I told myself
the words of an old grief,
my night forever cleft
from light.
Lament does not return,
slow canticle, to lips it left,
for there is nowhere for it to escape
the tapping of time lost,
deep in the heart.
Shattered dream, it becomes
small ash of fiercest flame.

I després el silenci,
petit, tan fràgil,
pell de tambor
que percudí la pluja.
Unes mans
molt suaus
davallaven la morta
cançó,
ninot penjat,
dels llavis de la follia
i la duien piadosament
al repòs de la llum.
Era portada en ales de paraules,
paraules mai no dites,
abelles resplendents.
I jo les seguia
fins al jardí llunyà,
i faig entrar l'eixam
endins de l'oblit,
i fonello ja per sempre el rusc.

And then the silence,
small, fragile
drumskin
hammered by the rain.
The softest
hands
loose the dead
song,
hanged doll,
from the lips of madness
and set it piously
to rest in light.
It was borne on wings of words,
words never said,
shimmering bees.
I followed them
as far as the distant garden,
led the swarm
into oblivion,
and now tamp the hive forever.

Abelles. Tot l'eixam
tancava dintre l'arna.
És el fonell del buc
de pedra molt pesada.

La terra del bancal
la son dels bous llaurava.
Espona has de bastir
de pedra perdurable.

Amb sang he volgut fer
una cançó de marbre.
La pluja l'esborrà,
paraula per paraula.

La llosa de l'oblit
a poc a poc va caure.
Ni el llarg plorar dels morts
mai més no podrà alçar-la.

Bees. The whole swarm
closed within the nest.
The tympan of the hive
is made of heavy stone.

The cows' sleep plowed
the fertile land.
Terraces you'll need
of everlasting rock.

With blood I tried to write
a marble song.
The rain erased it,
word by word.

The tombstone of oblivion
fell bit by bit.
Not even the long cry of the dead
will raise it up again.

Arços i grèvol,
oculta neu, prim aire
de tramuntana.
Hivern del mar: sol fràgil
damunt platges desertes.

Hawthorn and holly,
hidden snow, thin air
the north wind sends.
Winter at sea: fragile sun
above the empty beach.

II

Dansa grotesca de la mort

Horari lent de dolor.
L'ombra suprema davalla
fins al rebel. Faramalla,
màgia banal: antigalla.

A l'ull obert la claror
s'ha congelat en grisalla.
Un glop de sol. Requincalla
de plors fingits de canalla.

Pregària breu al Senyor
Déu Jesucrist embolcalla
amb dol extern la baralla
per quatre sous de xavalla.

Flames de ciris. Buidor.
Vetllen la rica sucalla.
Trist pensament ja tenalla
la pietosa brivalla:
"Malaguanyada mortalla!"

Grotesque Dance of Death

Slow timetable of grief.
The almighty shade descends
to the rebel. Banal magic,
flimflam: the same old stuff.

Before your eyes the light
has turned to frozen gray.
A splash of sun. Bric-a-brac,
sham tears that children shed.

A quick prayer to our Lord
Jesus Christ wraps the spat
in outside pain
for four mean cents.

Tapers flame. Emptiness.
Keep watch over the rich brew.
Sad thought already grips
the pious crowd:
"Accursed shroud!"

Viatge d'hivern

La pluja clama sempre
damunt la fortalesa de Déu,
perpò jo no responc sinó amb silenci,
perquè el temps ha passat.

Somric al gran missatge
d'aquelles hores. Només
sé ara que la sang
m'ha destruït el món.

Per una erta plana
de mar, de nit, camino
un hivern solitari.
No sé l'indret de l'illa
de l'esperança: només,
que sang que no he vessat
m'ha destruït el món.

Winter Journey

The rain still pounds
above God's fortress,
but I reply with silence,
for the time has passed.

I smile at the great message
of those hours. All
I know now is that blood
has wrecked my world.

At night, in lonely winter,
I walk a stiff plain
of the sea. I don't know
which way hope's island
lies: all I know is that
blood I did not shed
has wrecked my world.

Cançó de Tirèsias

Ara la mort em priva
dels meus ulls, per mirar-te.

Clamo, perdut, i capto.
M'ha fet orb. Com t'esguarda!

Fuges a tramuntana,
on et dius seguríssim.

Penses potser: "Tinc gossos,
guardo l'or, conec llibres.

Pot l'endeví saber-me
tan endins d'aquests somnis?"

Sí, ben semblant als altres:
rostre, camí, refugi.

Però la mort prenia
uns vells ulls i s'atansa.

Tiresias's Song

Now death takes my eyes
from me, to look at you.

I'm lost and blind. I shout.
She's made me blind. How she watches you!

You flee across the mountains
to where you say you are safe.

Perhaps you think: "I keep dogs,
stock gold, know books.

Can the soothsayer find me out
deep within these dreams?"

Yes, just like the others:
face, road, refuge.

But death takes
ancient eyes and draws near.

El posseït

Però el torb em priva
de seguir l'amor únic.
I aquestes mans que vetllen
el foc volen de sobte
urpejar, amb vivíssim
desig de sang, i foscos
udols esqueixen llavis
que varen dir paraules.
Sóc ja obsessiva trama
d'aràcnid, fred designi
de mal, mentre contemplo
només llot i una fressa
de ventres rèptils puja
de la nit absoluta
cap a l'esclat de l'odi.

The Possessed Man

But the uproar doesn't let me
follow single love.
These hands that watch
the fire are seized with a sudden
need to claw, a fierce
desire for blood, and dark
howls rip lips
that once said words.
Already I am obsessive
weft of arachnid, cold design
of evil, as I contemplate
only mud and a hiss
of reptile bellies rises
out of total night
into the flare of hate.

Petit eco en el Styx

Ara, desvetllat serpent,
anellant-me en secrets signes,
em perdia pels malignes
camins del meu pensament.
Presoner de mancament
que creix en un vell dolor,
negre riu dominador,
aigua de negat, t'emportes,
crit avall, record de mortes
esperances de claror.

Small Echo in the Styx

Now, a restless snake,
coiling in secret signs,
I lost my way in the malign
corridors of thought.
Prisoner of loss
that wells from an ancient grief,
black river riding high,
water of the drowned, you sweep
downscream all traces of the dead,
all hope of light.

Cançó de la vinguda de la tarda

Una a una,
en els meus ulls ordeno
les vides conegudes.

Casa, carena, barca,
ample respir de l'aigua,
clara rosa. Amb paraules
sempre noves vestia
la tarda ja nascuda.

La nua tarda,
que de la llum sortia
al mar i a la muntanya.

Song of Evening's Arrival

One by one
I assemble in my eyes
the lives I know.

House, hill, ship,
deep breath of water,
clear rose. With words
always new I clothe
the newborn evening.

Naked evening,
rising from the light
to the mountain and the sea.

Cançó del pas de la tarda

Entra la tranquil·la tarda
pel fosc camí de la mirada.

Enllà del mar ben treballat
pels bous del sol, endins del blat,
quan més perfecta mor la flor
a l'aire lleu, pel gran dolor
d'aquest camí de la mirada,
se'n va la tranquil·la tarda.

Song of Evening's Footsteps

Evening arrives
along the dark path of the eyes.

Beyond the sea tilled
by the oxen of the sun, within the wheat,
as each perfected flower dies
in the soft air, evening recedes
along the grieving
pathway of the eyes.

Cançó del triomf de la nit

On l'or acaba
tan lentament, banderes,
nit enlairada.

Escolta una remor
de moltes aigües:
amb el vent, contra tu,
cavalls salvatges.
Quan et sentis cridat
pels corns de caça,
ja per sempre seràs
del fosc reialme.

Ai, el vell arrelat
dolor que no té alba!

Song of Triumphant Night

Flags where the gold
slowly ends,
night unfurled.

Listen to the roar
of many waters:
with the wind, against you,
wild horses.
When you hear
the hunter's horn,
you will belong forever
to the realm of darkness.

Old rooted pain
that knows no dawn!

Prometeu

El somni de llibertat esdevé la cadena
que em lliga ja per sempre al meu cant dolorós.
M'he compadit dels homes, de la freda tristesa
de l'estrany temps dels homes endinsats en la mort,
i els portava cristall i cremor de paraules,
claroso noms que diuen els vells llavis del foc.
Àguila, vinguda del naixement del llamp,
d'on veus com és pensada la blancor de la neu,
cerca, per a la llum, la més secreta vida:
per al sol, palpitant, tota la nua vida.
Obriràs amb el bec eternament camins
a la sang que ofereixo com a preu d'aquest do.

Prometheus

The dream of liberty becomes the chain
that binds me now forever to my painful song.
I pitied men, the cold grief of the strange time
of men immersed in death,
and I brought them glass and blaze of words,
bright names spoken by old lips of fire.
Eagle, sprung from lightning's birth,
from where you see the way snow's whiteness is conceived,
seek, for the light, most secret life,
for the sun, trembling, all naked life.
With your beak you shall tear eternal paths
for the blood I offer as the price of this gift.

Des del mateix teatre

Sé com encara
en el record, intacte,
és el somriure.
Però les mans, ja cendra
o llum, on retrobar-les?

From the Theater Itself

I know the smile,
intact still
in memory.
But the hands, already ash
or light, who'll retrieve them?

El brau, en l'arena de Sepharad,
envestia l'estesa pell
i en fa, enlairant-la, bandera.
Contra el vent, aquesta pell
de toro, del brau cobert de sang,
és ja parrac espesseït per l'or
del sol, per sempre lliurat al martiri
del temps, oració nostra
i blasfèmia nostra.
Alhora víctima, botxí,
odi, amor, lament i rialla,
sota la closa eternitat del cel.

The bull, in the arena of Sepharad,
attacked the time-stretched skin,
unfurling it into a flag.
Against the wind, this bull's skin
slick with blood, rag
already thick with the sun's
gold, pledged forever to the martyrdom
of time, our prayer
and our blasphemy.
Now victim, hangman,
hate, love, laughter and lament
beneath the sky's eternal clasp.

Els nostres avis varen mirar,
fa molts anys,
aquest mateix cel
d'hivern, alt i trist,
i llegien en ell un estrany
signe d'emparança i de repòs.
I el més vell dels vianants
l'assenyalà amb el llarg
bastó de la seva autoritat,
mostrant-lo als altres,
i després indicà aquests camps
i va dir:
—Certament aquí descansarem
de tota la vastitud dels camins
de la Golah.
Certament aquí
m'enterrareu.

I eren també enterrats,
un a un, a Sepharad,
tots els qui amb ell arribaven,
i els fills i els néts,
fins a nosaltres.
Car prou sabem que molts
som encara escampats
en el vent i en la peregrinació
de la Golah.
Però ja no volem plorar

Our grandparents stared once,
many years ago,
at this same winter sky,
gray and high,
and read in it a strange sign
of sustenance and rest.
The oldest of the travelers
signalled with the long
staff of his authority
and then he pointed to these fields
and told the others:
"Surely it is here that we shall rest
from the vast highways
of the Golah.
Surely it is here
that you shall bury me."

And they too were buried
one by one in Sepharad,
all those who were with him then
and all their children, and their children too,
on down to ourselves.
For well we know that many of us
are still scattered
in the wind and wandering
of the Golah.
But we no longer want to mourn

més el temple
ni sofrir per l'infinit enyor
de la nostra ciutat.

Per això, quan algú
de tard en tard s'atansa
i amb un posat sever
ens pregunta:
"Per què us quedeu aquí,
en aquest país aspre i sec,
ple de sang?
No és certament aquesta
la millor terra que trobàveu
a través de l'ample
temps de prova
de la Golah,"
nosaltres, amb un lleu somriure
que ens apropa el record
dels pares i dels avis,
responem només:
—En el nostre somni, sí.

the temple
or suffer the immense longing
for our city.

Therefore, when someone
comes day after day
and gravely asks:
"What keeps you
in this harsh, arid,
blood-soaked land?
Surely it is not
the best land you could find
throughout the vast,
trying time of the Golah,"
with a slight smile
that reminds us of
our parents and our grandparents
we answer simply,
"In our dream it is."

Estiraven les ales de l'ocell solar,
per la façana el pugen cap a dalt.
El claven prou enlaire, reblen els claus.
Retrunyen martellades. A poc d'espai,
dits de botxins manobres el deixen ja
fix en el mur, immòbil. Ben aviat,
els ulls que porten dintre l'immens palau
de la claror pensada s'entelaran
de lenta mort petita. I esdevindrà
l'esglaiós sacrifici d'imperial
captiu que per llargs segles senyorejà
els cims, el cel, els somnis de Sepharad,
un barroer martiri de casolà
capó per a la festa del canvi d'any,
dolor de renegaire rat-penat.

They stretch the wings of the sun bird,   ·ר
hoist him up to the top of the facade.
They nail him high, with stinging blows.
The hammering resounds. Soon
the executioner's thick fingers
pin him to the wall. And soon
these eyes that hold vast palaces
of imagined light will cloud
with slow, miniature death. And then will come   ב
the dreadful sacrifice of the imperial
captive who for centuries ruled
the peaks, the sky, the dreams of Sepharad.
Humdrum martyrdom, homespun
capon for the New Year's feast,
anguish of blaspheming bat.

No ens preguntis, ignora quin tedi, quins llavis
de cansament limiten el trau, com deia la boca
sense repòs els mots de l'últim fred. Nosaltres
riem de por d'entendre del pallasso
que sols l'ànima es mor, només la mica d'aire.
El vell senglar combat atiant els ullals dels gossos
de la desemparança de la nit, al peu de l'arbre
solitari, tan nu, d'aquest penjat immòbil.
Ah, Sepharad! Els febles llums ara se'ns apagaven
del tot, mentre l'home perdut i gran fa una llarga
suca-mulla final de pensaments angoixosos
i es nega a poc a poc en el seu vi.

Don't ask us; better not to know what weariness, what lips,
surround the wound, or how the mouth, unceasing,
spoke words of final cold. We laugh with fear
to hear the clown say that the soul alone,
that scrap of air, is mortal.
The wild boar sets its tusks against the hounds
of unrelenting night, beneath the solitary
tree, stark naked, of this stiff hanged man.
Oh Sepharad! The flickering lights go out
forever while the lost, large man makes a long
final stew of anguished thoughts
and sinks, drowning, in his wine.

Diversos són els homes i diverses les parles,
i han convingut molts noms a un sol amor.

La vella i fràgil plata esdevé tarda
parada en la claror damunt els camps.
La terra, amb paranys de mil fines orelles,
ha captivat els ocells de les cançons de l'aire.

Sí, comprèn-la i fes-la teva, també,
des de les oliveres,
l'alta i snezilla veritat de la presa veu del vent:
"Diverses són les parles i diversos els homes,
i convindran molts noms a un sol amor."

People are many and many are their tongues,
and many names have run into a single love.

The old fragile silver becomes an afternoon
suspended in the glow above the fields.
In snares of a thousand gentle ears
the earth has caught the birds of the air's song.

Yes, understand and make yours
from the olive groves
the high, simple truth of the wind's trapped voice: <
"People are many and many are their tongues,
and many names are needed for a single love."

Verola el raïm, i ara de cop l'estesa
lentitud de l'estiu s'aixeca al davant,
com un mur, i ens imposava,
ulls endins, aquest estrany retorn,
i mirem caminant les clarors allunyades.
Vet aquí les vinyes, i els arbres, i el mar,
i nosaltres, encara, sota el cel de Sepharad.
Donarem un darrer nom a cada cosa,
quan facin vells records quasi una nova creació.
Prou saps que enllà ja no hi ha res, excepte
la quieta, freda, solitària, fosca
llum, graons i pous de llum, on les paraules
s'apaguen i es perdien a cavall del silenci.
Ressona el galop, ben al fons, el galop
per llargs carrers nocturns d'aigua molt negra,
i ens sentim pensats supremament en la por.

The grape reddens on the vine and suddenly
summer's vast slowness rises
like a wall, imposing
on our inner eye this strange return,
and as we walk we watch the distant lights.
Here are the vines, here the trees and the sea,
and here are we, still, beneath the sky of Sepharad.
We shall give each thing a final name
as old memory shapes an almost new creation.
You know too well that nothing lies beyond, except
the still, cold, solitary, dark
light, stairs and wells of light, where words
flicker and are lost, riders on the back of silence.
The gallop echoes far below, down
long nocturnal streets of blackest water,
and we feel ourselves supremely thought in fear.

Però tu te'n rius:
penses que l'aranya
sempre tindrà fil.

Em tornes mesell
i em deixes podrint-me
en aquest femer.

Has venut de franc
al drapaire tires
de la pell de brau.

Gos, la teva tos
voldria escurar-nos
fins al moll de l'os?

Ensenyem al fart
els nostres vells queixos
ja del tot xuclats.

Rebentes de tip,
mentre esdeveníem
cada cop més prims.

El genet estrany
dalla als camps de l'aire
fenc per al cavall.

But you laugh:
you think the spider always
will have thread.

You make me numb,
leaving me to fester
in this dung.

You sell the ragman
strips of bull's skin
for a song.

Dog, is your cough
supposed to scrape us
to the bone?

We show the fat man
our old jowls
all sucked in.

You're bursting at the seams
while we grow
thin.

The strange horseman
rakes his hay
from fields of air.

Envoltat de fum,
perds el món de vista
i t'acluques d'ulls.

Quan despertaràs,
la rialla als llavis
se t'estroncarà.

Wrapped in smoke,
you shut your eyes
and the world dims.

When you wake,
the laughter on your lips
will freeze in place.

A vegades és necessari i forçós
que un home mori per un poble,
però mai no ha de morir tot un poble
per un home sol:
recorda sempre això, Sepharad.
Fes que siguin segurs els ponts del diàleg
i mira de comprendre i estimar
les raons i les parles diverses dels teus fills.
Que la pluja caigui a poc a poc en els sembrats
i l'aire passi com una estesa mà
suau i molt benigna damunt els amples camps.
Que Sepharad visqui eternament
en l'ordre i en la pau, en el treball,
en la difícil i merescuda
llibertat.

Sometimes it is necessary and right
for a man to die for a people.
But a whole people must never die
for a single man:
remember this, Sepharad.
Keep the bridge of dialogue secured
and try to understand and love
the different minds and tongues of all your children.
Let the rain fall drop by drop on the fields
and the air cross the ample fields
like a soft, benevolent hand.
Let Sepharad live forever
in order and in peace, in work,
and in difficult, hard-won
liberty.

'Ix, 'Ixa, Elí, Elis!

Hem pujat el nostre crit a tu
i ens posàvem de puntetes per semblar més alts.
Ens hem vist en la nostra nuesa,
ens hem mirat en la nostra solitud
i hem engendrat després fills i filles,
al llarg de tot el tedi del nostre temps.
Ah, si raonem, quina rialla trista,
en negar-te en la niciesa dels nostres cors!
Ai, si t'estimem, quantes llàgrimes
fa vessar de seguida el nostre amor cruel!
I també hi ha la sang, la fatiga mil·lenària,
immensa, de la sang. Des de la sorra
d'aquest desert, des de l'amarga
profunditat del pou, et clamo
contra l'olor, contra el color, contra el voltor.
Sí, clamem contra la sang, nosaltres,
que hem vist els arbres i sabem prou bé
com el teu nom pot ser burla o silenci.

Ish, Isha, Eli, Elis!

We cried up to you
and stood on tiptoe to seem taller.
We have seen ourselves in our nakedness,
stared at ourselves in our solitude,
and gone on to sire sons and daughters
through all the terrible tedium of our time.
If we stopped to think, what sad laughter
for denying you within our hearts!
And if we love you, what tears
spill suddenly from our cruel love!
Then there's the blood, the vast millennial
exhaustion of the blood. From the sands
of this desert, from the bitter
depth of the well, I cry out to you
against the odor, against the color, against the vulture.
Yes, we cry out against the blood, we
who have seen the trees and who know too well
that your name can be mockery or silence.

—Recorda't de nosaltres,
per sempre allunyats de la llum de la barca,
privats dels camins del mar i de les ales.
Amb la terra esperàvem la pluja rara,
la set demanava una almoina clara.
La pluja venia i ens era contrària,
ens tancava enllà d'altes reixes d'aigua,
apagava el clam d'ombres ja penades.
Però amb els teus ulls nosaltres ploràvem
i ens fèiem arrel, l'arrel més amarga
d'aquest vell dolor d'amagades llàgrimes.
Plorem dintre teu, dins de les paraules,
en cada una de les teves paraules,
perquè ens recordis avui encara.

—El meu temps estrany el dol esborrava.
Molt a poc a poc la llosa va caure:
ni amb el vostre plany no podreu alçar-la.

—Moríem en tu o has mort amb nosaltres?
Ets aquí també, ja cançó acabada?
Si per tu sentim com el toc s'enlaira,
que fosc han sonat les fosques campanes!

"Remember us,
banned forever from the light of ships,
denied the paths of sea and wings.
With earth we waited for the rare rain.
Our thirst begged bright alms.
The rain arrived and was against us,
locking us in behind high gates of water,
drowning out the cries of the damned.
But we wept with your eyes and made ourselves
into roots, the bitter root
of that old grief of hidden tears.
We wept with you, within words,
within each word you spoke,
so that you'd still remember us today."

"Grief erased my strange time.
The tombstone fell so slowly
not even your lament can raise it."

"Did we die in you, or did you die with us?
Are you here too, finished song?
Through you we hear the tolling rise,
how dark the darkness of the bells!"

Petites cobles d'entenebrats

Fragments esotèrics en cadena, trobats en escrits de mal averany.

Els anys m'han entaforat
records de calaix de sastre
clepsa endins. Sento remor
de serpents de cascavell.

Temo que perdré la pell
a la fosca d'un racó
o daurat al socarrim,
convicte i confés del crim
de ser catòlic, burgès,
proletari, descregut,
monàrquic, republicà.
O perquè vaig trontollar
amb arrufades de nas
la moral d'un conegut.
M'enderroca un esternut,
i no goso ni piular.

Espòs difunt em deixà,
en assenyat testament,
paper de l'Ajuntament
i títols de capellà:
renda força sanejada,
segons càlculs trets abans
de la gran tamborinada.
Ara, pobreta de mi,
em trobo ben a l'escapça.

Small Couplets of the Damned

Esoteric fragments in chain form found in writings of ill omen.

The years have crammed
my skull with memories,
a messy drawer. I hear the roar
of rattlesnakes rush in.

I'm afraid I'll lose my skin
in some dark corner
or be roasted to a crisp,
having committed and confessed to the crime
of being Catholic, bourgeois,
proletarian, an unbeliever,
monarchist, Republican.
Or because I undermined
a friend's morale
by wrinkling my nose.
A sneeze undoes me,
so I'm mum.

Dead husband left a handsome sum
in his will duly notarized and signed,
Mayor's letterhead
and churchman's filigree,
according to the figures from
before the storm.
Now, poor thing,
I'm high and dry.

Ulls de damnat, de relapse,
vigilen el secret fil
d'aquest meu destí, tan vil,
que faré la ballaruga
a l'extrem d'una samuga.
Avanço per carrers bruts,
entremig de multituds,
disputant ossos a cans
tinyosos, plens de brians.

Furgo muntanyes de guants,
neguitós de descobrir
un dit de la mà de Déu.
Mentre cauen cóps de neu,
rego testos de safrà,
jaborandi, romeguera.
Confio que brostarà
una rara flor d'encant
la vetlla de Sant Joan,
amb virtuts d'herba gatera.

Em dic Salom, fill de Sinera.
Contemplo el buit, mirant enrera.
I, temps enllà, tan sols m'espera
desert, tristor d'hora darrera.

Eyes of the damned, who still defy,
watch the secret thread
of a destiny so dread
I'll dance a jig
at my rope's end.
I walk filthy streets
amid the throng,
fight mangy dogs
over a bone.

I ransack piles of gloves,
eager to find
a finger from God's hand.
While cups of snow land on the ground
I water pots of saffron,
blackberry, and jaborandi.
And trust that a rare flower
with catnip's strength
will bloom before the evening of Saint John.

I'm called Salom, Sinera's son.
I contemplate what's done and gone.
Beyond time, emptiness alone
awaits, the sadness of the final hour.

Llibre dels morts

Mira que passes sense saviesa
pel vell camí fressat, tan sols un cop,
i que la veu de sobte cridarà
el secret nom que porta en tu la mort.
No tornaràs. Recorda, no t'apartis,
mentre fas via, del que tan senzill
és d'estimar: aquest blat i la casa,
el blanc senyal de barca dins el mar,
el lent or de l'hivern ajaçat a les vinyes,
l'ombra d'un arbre damunt l'ample camp.
Oh, sobretot estima la sagrada
vida de l'arbre i la remor del vent
a les branques que s'alcen vers la llum!

Book of the Dead

Look, you walk the old threshed path
in ignorance, just once,
and a voice suddenly cries out
the secret name death wears in you.
You will not return. Remember, do not stray
as you go, from what is easiest
to love: this wheat and this house,
the white sign of a ship on the sea,
winter's slow gold draped over the vines,
the shadow of a tree across the ample fields.
But above all love the sacred
life of the tree and wind's roar
in the branches rising toward the light!

El vell estimat Brueghel
ho ha contat així

Mentre la llum encara
és als camps i retornen
de la lenta llaurada
els bous a l'establia,
ulls de molts cecs esguarden
com són fetes les balles
per dansadors que calça
d'esclops la riallera
comare mort.

Oh, fugir on no fossin
tan nuament sabudes,
tan closes dintre l'ordre
d'aquestes llises nines,
les diferents postures
dels meus peus a la dansa!

Sac de gemecs. M'emporto
la dona i la cullera
i unes dents esmolades
de llop, amb la certesa
de perdre'm ja per sempre
al mig de la febreta
dels giravolts. I sento
com esdevinc tenebra
empresonada al fons
de les buides mirades.

Old Brueghel Told It Thus

While the light still
lies on the fields and the cows
return to the fold
from the long ploughing,
eyes of many blind men watch
the whirling dancers grinning
mother death
has shod in clogs.

Oh, to flee where
the different patterns
of my footsteps in the dance,
so tightly shut within the order
of these supple girls,
were not so nakedly exposed!

Old crank. I take
my wife and my spoon
and a few sharp
wolf's teeth, knowing
I will lose myself forever
in the feverish
turns. And I feel myself
becoming darkness
trapped within
the empty stares.

III

Remor de cops d'aixada, no la sents?
Rera les altes tanques de paret.
Sense repòs, però molt lentament,
enllà de la cleda contínua del temps.

Arrencaven els ceps, han cremat els sarments,
damunt la terra bona s'estenia l'erm.
Pel serpent del rial arrosseguem
passos neguitosos d'aquests peus de vell.

La saviesa clamava al guaret,
a les canyes seques que movia el vent:
"Contempla't en mi com esdevens
aconseguida mort de tu mateix."

Ajupits en l'ombra, caven comparets
a les despullades vinyes de l'hivern.
No hi ha llum per tota la buidor del cel.
Només uns cops d'aixada al fons del fred.

Don't you hear the sound the hoe makes
beyond the steep rising walls?
Never stopping, but so slow,
beyond time's endless fold.

They pulled up the vines and burned the roots.
Barrenness settled in on the good earth.
We haul this old man's restless steps
along the snaking riverbed.

Wisdom shouted in the fallow field,
in the dry windswept shoots:
"Behold yourself in me, as you become
your own accomplished death."

Crouched in the shade, hired hands
uproot winter's naked vines.
The whole empty sky is dark.
Just the sound the hoe makes in the deepening cold.

Ets en el teu hivern, i aquest fred de la terra,
desvetllat pel magall, sorgit a poc a poc,
puja de cada clot i s'estén i cobria
de closques de secs cargolins el cansament del mur.
Ah, tants petits esforços ja buidats de sentit,
tan lluny encara, i per sempre, del premi dels vidres
que guarden el dret de la son i la burla de l'amo!
Però bolla una mata de peix en l'enfosquida mar,
on sé més l'espessor de sapes i d'anquines,
i la mica de vent s'apropa fins al guaret i deixa
a penes un tel de recordada boira en el prim fonoll.

You are in your winter, and this coldness of the earth
the spade pries free rises bit by bit,
flies from each hollow and spreads
dry snail shells across the tired wall.
So many tiny efforts stripped of sense,
so far away still, and forever, from the prize of the glass
that holds the right to sleep and the master's mockery!
But a school of fish roils the dark sea,
where I know best the thickness of sharks and eels,
and a lick of wind rolls to the fallow's edge and leaves just
the barest film of remembered fog on the thin fennel stalks.

He caminat estances de la casa
de la destral del llamp.
Perquè no té finestres,
no podia saber.
Perquè no hi ha cap porta,
no en podia fugir.
Enllà dels passadissos sense llum
avança contra mi un terrible plor,
un plany elemental per altes prades,
per lliures vents i boscos i la nit
ampla i oberta sota les estrelles.
En un extrem perill de mort, em sento molt
germà d'aquell dolor que ja s'atansa,
orb i enemic.
Aleshores, quan la sang
és escampada amb ira per la roja tenebra,
esdevinc justificat, home sencer.
I diuen els meus llavis,
nascudes del coratge, del compassiu somriure,
obrint-me finalment l'únic pas de sortida,
unes poques, fràgils, clares
paraules de cançó.

I have walked the rooms of the house
of the axe of lightning.
Because it has no windows
I could not know.
Because there is no door
I could not escape.
Beyond the lightless corridors
a terrible lament came toward me,
an elemental cry borne through high meadows,
free winds and forests and the night
vast and open underneath the stars.
In extreme peril of death, I feel myself
a brother to the coming pain,
my blind enemy.
Then, when blood
is spilled with rage across the reddened dusk,
I am justified, a simple man.
And my lips, opening at last
my only path of escape, speak,
born of courage, of a compassionate smile,
a few bright, fragile
words of song.

Diré del vell foc i de l'aigua.
Si crema molt la neu,
glaçava més la flama.

Diré de l'espasa i de l'aigua.
Si m'ha ferit la font,
em guarirà l'espasa.

Diré de l'ocell i de l'aigua.
Si llum de cims al riu,
fosca de terra l'ala.

Diré de la rosa i de l'aigua:
la mort de la mar fa
la flor més perdurable.

Diré dels meus ulls i de l'aigua.
Si tot ho mira el llac,
jo tinc les nines blanques.

Dic la pluja, la pluja, la pluja clara
i el plor de l'endinsat
sense retorn per l'aigua.
Dic el nom del no-res
enllà del fons de l'aigua.

I shall speak of the old fire and of water.
If snows burns much,
flame is more chilling.

I shall speak of the sword and of water.
If the spring has hurt me,
the sword shall heal me.

I shall speak of the bird and of water.
If mountain-light the river,
earth-dark the wing.

I shall speak of the rose and of water:
the sea's death makes
the flower more enduring.

I shall speak of my eyes and of water.
If the lake sees all,
the pupils of my eyes are white.

I speak the rain, the rain, the bright rain
and the tears of one turned inward on himself
who cannot return by water.
I speak the name of no-thing
beyond the farthest water.

Pel meu mirall, si vols, passen rares semblances

Davant el meu últim mirall, en veure'm
sencer, malalt, potser acabat,
potser damnat, tan pàl·lid,
vaig dir molt lentament clares paraules,
belles, fràgils, altes, les més nobles
que trobava en la foscor del meu record.
Des de sempre, però, allí hi havia
grasses, molles, llefiscoses bèsties,
que dels racons venien fins als llavis,
a rosegar-me els mots mentre naixien:
no sents encara la remor profunda
de pergamí, d'ossos trencats, de vidre?
I al mirall, entretant, es reflectia
a poc a poc una perversa imatge,
el signe de la qual podràs entendre,
si fas també, com jo, l'estranya prova
d'esguardar el teu bon fons, qualsevol hora,
tot intentant de nou una impossible,
inútil creació per la paraula.

Strange Forms, If You Will, Appear in My Mirror

Before my final mirror, seeing myself
complete, ill, done for perhaps,
perhaps damned, and pale,
I slowly spoke a few clear words,
beautiful, fragile, uplifting, the noblest
words I could find in the dark of memory.
But ever since I can remember it's been full
of fat, soft, viscous beasts
that crept from corners to my lips,
nibbling at my words as they took form:
don't you hear still the deep shuddering
of parchment, broken bones, glass?
And in the mirror, meanwhile,
a perverse image slowly appeared,
whose sign you will understand
if, like me, you attempt the strange feat
of staring into your own depths
as once again you attempt the impossible,
useless act of creating through the word.

El vent

Job 2:13.
Homenatge a Pablo Neruda.

Savis, molt cauts, des dels seus cors de glaç,
els vells s'han atansat a poc a poc
fins al mateix llindar del sofriment.
Callats, experts en esglaons del plany,
set dies i set nits van meditant
com furgaran després, sense cap risc,
els crims secrets de l'enemic leprós.
Altius, severs, recitaran lliçons,
en versos escandits amb art antic,
difícils, rars, perfectes, del tot buits:
l'ordit del seny contra l'injustament
sollat, tan despullat per un poder
estès per l'or amb les raons del foc.
Però s'aixecarà d'enllà dels cims
cremats de neu el cant profund del mort,
el vent advers a les presons de llum.
I quan serà damunt les deus del mar,
ens hem d'alliberar per sempre més
dels pous escarpellats per llargues pors,
arquers amb ell en l'amplitud del vol.

The Wind

Job 2:13
Homage to Pablo Neruda.

Wise, watchful, the old men inched
from their frozen hearts
to the very edge of suffering.
Silent, expert in the steps of grief,
for seven days and seven nights they meditate
on how to forage without risk
in the leprous enemy's secret crimes.
Haughty, severe, they call out their lessons
in lines scanned with ancient art,
difficult, rare, perfect, completely blank:
the warp of sense against one wrongly
stained, stripped by a force fire's reason
shuttles through the gold with arguments of fire.
But beyond the peaks ablaze with snow
death's deepest song will rise,
the wind that pounds the jails of light.
And when it's high above the ocean's source,
we shall be freed forever
from the wells dug by long fear,
archers on the broad sweep of its flight.

Inici de càntic en el temple

A Raimon, amb el meu agraït aplaudiment.
Homenatge a Salvat-Papasseit.

Ara digueu: "La ginesta floreix,
arreu als camps hi ha vermell de roselles.
Amb nova falç comencem a segar
el blat madur i, amb ell, les males herbes."
Ah, joves llavis desclosos després
de la foscor, si sabíeu com l'alba
ens ha trigat, com és llarg d'esperar
un alçament de llum en la tenebra!
Però hem viscut per salvar-vos els mots,
per retornar-vos el nom de cada cosa,
perquè seguíssiu el recte camí
d'accés al ple domini de la terra.
Vàrem mirar ben al lluny del desert,
davallàvem al fons del nostre somni.
Cisternes seques esdevenen cims
pujats per esglaons de lentes hores.
Ara digueu: "Nosaltres escoltem
les veus del vent per l'alta mar d'espigues."
Ara digueu: "Ens mantindrem fidels
per sempre més al servei d'aquest poble."

Beginning of Canticle in the Temple

To Raimon, with my grateful applause.
Homage to Salvat-Papasseit.

Now say: "The broom tree blooms,
everywhere the fields are red with poppies.
With new scythes we'll thresh
the ripened wheat and weeds."
Ah, young lips parting after dark,
if you only knew how dawn
delayed us, how long we had to wait
for light to rise in the gloom!
But we have lived to save your words,
to return you the name of every thing,
so that you'd stay on the straight path
that leads to the mastery of earth.
We looked beyond the desert,
plumbed the depth of our dreams,
turned dry cisterns into peaks
scaled by the long steps of time.
Now say: "We hear the voices
of the wind on the high sea of crested grain."
Now say: "We shall be ever faithful
to the people of this land."

Vols d'ànecs salvatges

A Lola Trullàs.

A l'últim esglaó
de l'escala corcada,
tot sol en el llindar
de la buida cabana,
l'ajaçat cansament
d'aquest cor centenari.

Miren amb fred esguard
uns ulls que van a cloure's.

—És més vella que jo
la fusta del recer.
L'aixecava quan era
jove i fort, ho recordo,
per als pares, la dona
i els molts fills que tindríem.
Ara són només ombres
allunyades de morts.

Arran dels peus s'atansa
l'aiguamoll, abans camps
que lents cobles llauraven.
De tan breu, del llarg somni
no comprenc el sentit.
Però ja puc somriure,
sense desigs ni por.

Pel cel baix de l'hivern
passen vols, cap al sud,

Flights of Wild Geese

To Lola Trullás.

On the last step
of the rotted stairs,
alone at the threshold
of the empty hut,
lies the weariness
of this century-old heart.

Eyes that are about to close
gaze with a cold stare.

"The wood of this shed
is older than myself.
I built it when I
was young and strong,
for my parents, I recall, for my wife
and the many children we would have.
Now they are all just
distant shadows of the dead.

At my feet lies
the swamp, once fields
plowed by slow teams.
I can't understand
long dreams so fast.
But already I can smile
without desire or fear.

Across the low winter sky
flights of white wild geese

de blancs ànecs salvatges.
Amb ells me n'aniré,
a la fi deslliurat.

Quan sigui primavera,
unes mans piadoses
allisaran la pols
al desert del sorral.

head south.
I join them,
free at last.

When spring comes
pious hands
will smooth the dust
on the empty sands."

Aquesta tristesa, immensa, glaçadora,
que plana des de sempre damunt nostre,
fa que sentim proper l'acabament d'un món.
Però qui sap si algú, des del mar de naufragi,
un dia guanyarà la clara riba
i ordenarà de nou el pas afermat
pels oberts i dreturers camins.
Aleshores serà potser comprès el cant
que s'elevà i amb molt dolor venia
del cor mateix d'aquesta nit.

This vast, chilling grief
that always hovers overhead
makes the end of a world feel close.
Who knows, though, but that someone, some day,
will reach the bright shore from the shipwrecked sea
and set off with firm stride
down the open, righteous roads.
Perhaps then someone will make sense of the song
that rose and came suffering
from the heart of this night.

Sentit a la manera de Salvador Espriu

He de pagar el meu vell preu, la mort,
i avui els ulls se'm cansen de la llum.
Baixats amb mancament tots els graons,
m'endinsen pel domini de la nit.

Silenciós, m'alço rei de la nit
i em sé servent dels homes de dolor.
Ai, com guiar aquest immens dolor
al clos de les paraules de la nit?

Passen el vent, el triomf, el repòs,
per rengles d'altes flames i d'arquers.
Presoner dels meus morts i del meu nom,
esdevinc mur, jo caminat per mi.

I em perdo i sóc, sense missatge, sol,
enllà del cant, enmig dels oblidats
caiguts amb por, només un somni fosc
del qui sortí dels palaus de la llum.

Felt in the Style of Salvador Espriu

I'll have to pay my old price, death,
and today my eyes are tired from the light.
In loss I have descended all the steps,
and they plunge me into the domain of night.

Silent, I rise up king of the night
and know myself the servant of all men who grieve.
But how to lead this immense grief
into the safety of the words of night?

The wind, triumph, and repose
pass through rows of leaping flames and archers.
Prisoner of my dead and of my name,
I become a wall, myself walked by myself.

I lose myself and am alone, with no message,
beyond song, among the forgotten,
those who fell in fear, merely a dark dream
of one who stepped from the palaces of light.

Amb lent dolor esdevé somni fosc
aquella llum dels altíssims palaus.
I el temps l'escampa pel record, ja flor desfeta
als dits aspres de pluja del meu extrem hivern.
Miro tota la nit i sento el cor
vastíssim de la terra, el maternal
respir fangós que guarda el vinent blat.
Arribaran demà tranquil·les hores,
obertes ales amples dels ocells
duran al camp les grans calmes d'estiu.
Hi haurà potser molt piadosos arbres
d'ombres esteses damunt secs camins.
Però jo, que sabia el cant secret de l'aigua,
les lloances del foc, de la gleva i del vent,
sóc endinsat en obscura presó,
vaig davallar per esglaons de pedra
al clos recinte de llises parets
i avanço sol a l'esglai del llarg crit
que deia per les voltes el meu nom.

With slow pain the light
of the high palaces becomes dark dream.
Time scatters it through memory, flower already spent
in the harsh rain-fingers of my fierce winter.
Awake all night, I feel the earth's
vast heart, the motherly, muddy
breath that watches over the ripening wheat.
Tomorrow gentle hours will arrive,
broad open wings of birds will bring
the large calm of summer to the fields.
Perhaps pious trees of darkness
will lean across dry paths.
But I who knew the water's secret song,
the praise of fire, sod and wind,
am held deep in a dark jail,
I descended steps of stone
to the closed enclave of smooth walls,
and I advance alone to the terror of the long cry
that sends my name ringing through the vaults.

Assentiré de grat, car només se'm donà
d'almoina la riquesa d'un instant.

Si podien, però, durar
la llum parada, l'ordre clar
dels xiprers, de les vinyes, dels sembrats,
la nostra llengua, el lent esguard
damunt de cada cosa que he estimat!

Voltats de por, enmig del glaç
de burles i rialles d'albardans,
hem dit els mots que són la sang
d'aquest vell poble que volem salvar.

No queden solcs en l'aigua, cap senyal
de la barca, de l'home, del seu pas.
L'estrany drapaire omplia el sac
de retalls de records i se'n va,
sota la fosca pluja, torb enllà,
pels llargs camins que s'esborren a mar.

I'll gladly go along, for all the alms
I had were the riches of a moment.

If only, though, this stopped light
could last, the bright order
of the cypresses, the vineyards and the fields,
our tongue and the slow gaze
above each thing I've loved.

Ringed by fear, amid the ice
of taunts and the laughter of buffoons,
we have said the words that are the blood
of this old people we would save.

Not a furrow in the sea, not a trace
of the ship, the man, or of his step.
The strange ragman fills his sack
with scraps of memory and disappears
beneath the dark rain, beyond the storm,
down long paths that blur into the sea.

Ofrenat a Cèrber

He donat la meva vida a les paraules
i m'he fet lenta pastura d'aquesta fam de gos.
Ah, guardià, caritat per als ossos
car ja t'arribo sense gens de carn!
Vaig enfonsar les mans en l'or misteriós
del meu vell català i te les mostro
avui, sense cap guany, blanques de cendra
del meu foc d'encenalls, i se m'allunya
per la buidor del cap el so del vidre fràgil.
Ara ballo amb dolor, perquè riguin les goles,
per obtenir l'aplaudiment dels mil lladrucs,
i em coronen amb un barret de cascavells.

Offering to Cerberus

I have given my whole life to words,
chewed this dog-hunger into a long meal.
Have mercy, sentry, on these bones,
for I arrive without a scrap of flesh!
I plunged my hands into the mysterious gold
of my beloved Catalan and hold them out
to you today empty of gain, white with ash
from my own fire, as the sound of fragile glass
recedes in the chasm of my head.
I dance in pain to make them laugh,
to win their barked applause,
and in the end they crown me with a jester's cap.

Knowles, el penjat, s'ho mira a cinc pams de la branca

És llàstima, bonica, que no t'hagis
gaudit avui d'aquesta meva força
darrera, de l'alegre dansa
del teu humil i segur servidor.
Passen amunt del cel lentíssims núvols,
i el vell escarabat, i veus estranyes
del vent, i moltes hores buides,
quan sóc fora del temps.
Després vindran els corbs, als quals agraden
els ulls, sobretot: abans de perdre'ls,
assenyat ballarí, mira, mira
aquest teu món, l'estimada, petita,
senzilla terra que tan bé domines
des de l'altura d'una fràgil branca.

Knowles, the Hanged Man, Looks Around from Five Spans Beneath the Branch

It's a shame, dear, that you weren't
here today to see my final
show, your faithful and humble
servant's happy dance.
Such slow clouds cross the sky,
and the old beetle, and the wind's
strange speech, and all the empty hours
when I am outside time.
Later the crows will come, who love
eyes most. Look hard, wise dancer,
before you give them up. Gaze, gaze
on this world of yours, this small, beloved,
simple land you see so well
from high on your fragile branch.

Just abans de laudes

Benignament sóc ara guiat
enllà del vell origen de les aigües,
on ja no sento la contínua font.
Quan els purs llavis reposin, cansats
de la vigília del tercer nocturn,
començarà l'ocell la clarosa lloança.
Jo, que moro i sé
la solitud del mur i el caminant,
et demano que em recordis avui,
mentre te'n vas amb les sagrades hores.

Just Before Lauds

Benignly I am led now
past the waters' ancient source
to where I can no longer hear the continual font.
When the pure lips rest, weary
from the watch of the third night,
the bird will launch its limpid praise.
I, who am dying and who know
the solitude of the wall and the passerby,
ask you to remember me today
as you disappear with the sacred hours.

Terra Negra

Reposa del camí. Sota l'ull d'or,
el regne és infinit. A la planura
de calma i solitud, el vent s'adorm.

Riu amunt, entre murs de desert,
ve la barca del déu. Mil estendards
flamegen en els pals, radiants de sol.
Sacerdots remadors canten vells himnes
al senyor de la mort, mentre fereixen
el llot, lee aigües grasses.

Aquesta llum, la pau d'aquest llarg dia,
són teves, caminant, si l'ampla terra
del blat etern et crida pel teu nom.

Black Land

Rest from your trip. Beneath the golden eye
the kingdom stretches forth forever. On the plain
of calm and solitude the wind drifts off to sleep.

Upriver, between desert walls,
the god's ship draws near. A thousand banners
flutter on the masts, ablaze with sun.
Rower priests sing ancient anthems
to the lord of death, as they pierce
the mud, the swollen waves.

This light, the peace of this long day,   `ר
are yours, traveler, if the vast earth
of eternal wheat cries out to you by your own name.   ג

IV

He deixat endarrera el sorral i la barca,
i la mar grunyia molt apagadament a la meva esquena,
allunyat gos foll d'un antic malson.
Camino amb esforç muntanyes amunt
i avanço per rengles i rengles de flames,
alimares de benvinguda de la nit.
Sento enllà una remor que s'atansa,
lliure galop de cavalls a les prades altes
que veig verdejar passats els límits del darrer bosc.
Perquè ja és de dia.
M'arriba de sobte la claror d'aquest nou dia
que esdevindrà plenitud del meu somni feliç.

I have left behind the sand and the ship,
and the muffled growl of the sea at my back,
mad dog of an ancient nightmare.
With great effort I ascend the slope,
advancing through row upon row of flames,
beacons of welcome in the night.
Up ahead I hear a sound approach,
broad gallop of horses in the high fields
greening above the edge of the last woods.
It is already day.
Suddenly I feel the brightness of this new day
that will become the fullness of my happy dream.

Com avui tu, i fins com tu, també, l'endinsat en demà,
aixecàvem ahir damunt la humida arena
castells de joc que sempre la mar d'estiu esborra
amb la seva ampla, contínua, mansa llengua de gos.
Som encara al sorral, i passen ran de les ones
xiscles i fum de trens esbalandrats de càrrega,
vers el nord o cap al sud, i s'allunyen per camps
estranys i del tot closos al lent amor dels ulls.
Ombres de guaites, des de la Torre dels Encantats,
vetllen l'injust repòs dels erigits en amos
de les més tristes hores. Furguem cercant la sang
del cor del pou ben agostat dels somnis,
amb llargs pals punxeguts de vells captaires.
Ara les petites muntanyes que s'alcen a ponent
es posen una a una mantellines de boira
i entraven en corrua pel gran portal del vespre,
a poc a poc, car toco pel nostre temps ja mort.

Like you today, and like you too, burrowed in tomorrow,
yesterday on the wet sand we built
castles that the summer sea always erases
with its wide, ceaseless, gentle dog-tongue.
We are still there on the strand, and beside the waves
pass the shrieks and smoke of trains cockeyed with freight,
heading north or south, as they disappear across
strange fields, completely closed to the slow love of eyes.
From the Tower of the Enchanted, shadows of sentries
watch the unjust sleep of those set up as masters
of the saddest hours. With an old beggar's long, sharp staff
we seek the blood at the heart of the parched well of dreams.
Now one by one the small mountains ranged against the dusk
don shawls of fog and pass slowly
through the great gate of the setting sun,
for I toll our time already dead.

Brins de paraules, filagarses
d'un mot a miques i a bocins,
no ens fan profit. Ventres endins,
botxinejaven becs de garses,
a la recerca del tresor
de cada tros. Xisclem a cor,
tips de passar, només comparses
privats de sou i son, a farses
dels llargs teatres de la nit,
fam en escenes de convit.

Threads of words, unravelings
of meaning split and cracked
do us no good. Geese claw
our gut to find the treasure
hidden in each crumb. Unpaid
walk-ons without lines, playing farces
in the long theaters of the night,
let's scream our hearts out.
We're sick of starving
in the banquet scenes.

Per quin camí et pot ferir la llum
i amb dard mortal abatre't del cavall?
Quan ets cremor, no veus l'ofec del fum
que al teu davant et priva del mirall.
Et sents llavor, espasa, clam, estrall,
i fas de tu mateix un llarg escrit.
Creuràs potser que tens ja l'esperit
guardat en pau dins el recer del nom.
Allí l'esglai et sap també, i el dit
raspa records, triomfs, tot el neguit
de salvament, i amb el desdeny d'un crit
t'entra, esborrat, al clos ball de tothom.

On what path can light wound you
and with mortal dart strike you from your horse?
When you are fire you can't see the smoke
that clogs the space between you and the mirror.
You feel yourself becoming seed, sword, havoc, scream,
you make yourself into an endless text.
Perhaps you think you can protect   ]
the spirit in the safety of the word.
But terror sniffs you out, a finger scrapes
at memories and triumphs, the whole yearning
for salvation, and with a scornful shout
enters you, erased, into the closed dance of everyone.

Com m'encercla el bosc!
Amaga'm dels arbres
de la meva por.

M'allunyes per la nit
de l'orb captaire:
endins he de sentir
temences d'alba?

Em sé presa segura
d'aquesta caça.
Quan cobris la despulla,
a qui portar-la?

Esdevinc, a l'hora clara,
nua ferida de prima llança.
Ja la gran set de tu
s'apaga en la meva ànima.

How the woods surround me!
Hide me from the trees
of dread.

You lead me through the night
of the blind beggar:
deep within am I to fear
the dawn?

I know myself the sure prey
of this chase.
When you claim the carcass,
for whom will it be?

In this bright hour I become
the naked wound of the fine lance.
Already my great thirst for you ⊃
is slaked within my soul.

Sense cap nom ni símbol,
ran dels xiprers, dessota
un poc de pols sorrenca,
endurida de pluges.
O que l'oratge escampi
la cendra per les barques
i els solcs dibuixadíssims
i la llum de Sinera.
Claror d'abril, de pàtria
que mor amb mi, quan miro
els anys i el pas: viatge
al llarg de lents crepuscles.

Without name or symbol,
beside the cypresses, beneath
a handful of dusty sand,
hard with rain.
Let the tempest strew
this ash over the boats
and deep-etched furrows
and Sinera's light.
Light of April, of the land
that dies with me when I contemplate
the footsteps and the years: journey
across slow dusks.

Elles demanen sols ajut
per acomplir la pietat
d'ungir d'aromes aquell cos
que dins el vas saben posat.

"Quins dits mourien
el gran pes de la llosa,
quan és l'alba? Que vinguin
a consolar-nos
de la buidor vetllada
unes veus compassives."

Del tot immòbils, amb espant
miren, escolten i després
ja se'n tornaven a ciutat.
Però la qui l'estima més
sent un subtil dolor sobtat
quand perd, veient-lo al seu davant,
fins alambins de soledat.

All they ask is help
in the pious act
of rubbing aromatic oils on the corpse
they know lies in the tomb.

"Whose hands will move
the stone's great weight
at dawn? Oh let
compassionate voices
console us
in the violent dark . . ."

Completely still, in dread
they watch, hear, and then
head back to the city.
But the one who loves him most
feels a sudden subtle pain when,
seeing him before her, the fine threads
of solitude are loosed.

Díptics de vivents

Del mar han de salvar-me
potser un vers, unes clares
paraules, mentre valguin
tota la meva vida.
Però temo que sigui
tan poc preu, que demano
a la fam dels captaires
una mica d'almoina:
pregueu per mi, pel somni
del captiu, per la nostra
sofrença, pels qui porten
els senyals de la cendra
i mort al cor i als llavis.

Diptych of the Living

From the sea I will be saved
perhaps, by poetry, a few
bright words that stand
for my whole life.
But I fear I ask so
small a price, that
I must seek alms
from beggars' hunger:
pray for me, for the dream
of the captive, for our
suffering, for all who bear
the sign of ash and death
in their hearts and on their lips.

No naixerà cap marbre
d'eternitzades ones
ni s'alçaran vols d'àngels
d'imaginats imperis.
Car és vingut de sobte
el temps dolent, i em porten
veus de records, per buides
estances de Sinera,
fins al guaita de l'alba,
xiprer que sap l'incendi
del mar i d'aquest núvol.

There will be no marble
of eternal waves,
nor will the angels of imaginary
empires take flight.
For suddenly hard times
have come, and remembered
voices bear me through
Sincera's empty rooms
to the sentinel of dawn,
cypress that knows the conflagration
of the sea and of this cloud.

Omnis fortasse moriar

El vespre és ple de sang, i no sé quin combat
magnifica el llarg plany del ponent, rera els cims.
Del fons d'uns ulls de cec he vist com surt el gos
maligne de la nit i corre pels camins
amplíssims de la por, lladrant la meva mort.
Oh, l'ocell que no canta, el bosc silenciós,
adormit príncep, vent! Ara cauré tot sol
i no seré més nom, ni record, ni dolor.
Escolto com se'n van aquelles clares veus
de la fulla i de l'aigua, estima l'últim cor,
a poc a poc em sento agermanat al fang.

Omnis Fortasse Moriar

The dusk is filled with blood and an unknown combat
magnifies the long moan of the setting sun behind the peaks.
From the depths of a blind man's eyes I've seen
the cursed dog of night scuttle the wide
paths of fear, howling my death.
Bird that doesn't sing, silent wood,
sleeping prince, wind! I shall fall alone now
and there be nothing left of me, not name, memory or pain.
I listen to the ebb of the bright voices
of leaves and water, love the last heart,
feel myself becoming slowly brothered to the mud.

Vinc a la nua
sequedat de la terra.
Sóc ja silenci
aprofundit. M'allunyo
d'una pols enlairada.

I have come to the naked
thirst of earth.
Already I have become
deep silence. Behind me,
a whirl of dust.

Però en la sequedat arrela el pi
crescut des d'ella cap al lliure vent
que ordeno i dic amb unes poques lletres
d'una breu i molt noble i eterna paraula:
m'alço vell tronc damunt la vella mar,
ombrejo i guardo el pas del meu camí,
reposa en mi la llum i encalmo ja la nit,
torno la dura veu en nu roquer del cant.

But in thirst the pine takes root,
leaps high toward the free wind
that I command and name with a few letters
from a brief, noble and eternal word:
old trunk, I rise above the ancient sea,
shadow and protect my route.
In me light rests and night is stilled,
I turn the hard voice into naked rock of song.

Eterna, noble, una paraula
en l'arrelada sequedat.
Ara, llum vell, ets apagat,
i ja ningú no seu a taula.
La veritat ens sembla faula,
es romp al nu roquer del cant.
En trossejats vents de l'espant
dansem el boig i la barjaula.
Alliberats, ens hem lliurat,
sota podrits dits de mesell,
al ball del crim. Volta el penell,
mai no parem, car l'amo és ell.
Endins del glaç d'uns ulls d'ocell,
aguait de forques, dels alçats
braços dels arbres dels penjats.

Eternal, noble, one word
in the deep-rooted thirst.
Now, old light, you've gone out,
and no one sits at table.
Truth strikes us as a fable,
breaks against the naked rock of song.
In the splintered winds of dread,
madman and wench, we spin headlong.
Set free, we deliver ourselves up
beneath the leper's rotten thumbs
to the dance of crime. The weathervane hums,
but we don't stop, he calls the shots.
In the icy stare of a bird's eye
a gallows waits, the upflung
arms of hanged men's trees.

Acaba aquí el viatge. Quan baixo de la barca,
sabia a ulls clucs com és al meu davant,
sempre pujat per cabres i per mates
d'espígol, de fonoll, de llet de bruixa
que a penes mouen aquelles primes mans
de l'ora quieta desvetllada al cim, el Mal Temps.
Límits estrictes d'una vella terra:
el seguici dels xiprers rera el carro del sol
que se'n va trontollant pels llargs i secs rials
i feia, en tramuntar, de la petita carena
llum i llunyania de l'horitzó de ponent.
He donat la meva vida pel difícil guany
d'unes poques paraules despullades.
He vist la meva vida com un mur
en el silenci de la tarda i el seu pas.

Here the voyage ends. When I step off the boat
I know with my eyes closed what lies before me:
steep with goats, thick
with milkweed, lavender and fennel
barely ruffled by the thin hands
of the peak's still, wakeful breeze: Rough Weather.
Strict limits of an old land:
the train of cypresses behind the sun chariot
that pounds the long, dry roads
and setting, turns the tiny hill
into the blaze and distance of the evening sky.
I have given my life for the hard prize ⌐
of a few bare words.
I have seen my life like a wall
in the silence of the afternoon and of its passing. ⌐

Quan et deturis
on el meu nom et crida,
vulgues que dormi
somniant mars en calma,
la claror de Sinera.

When you stop
where my name cries out to you,
wish me a deep sleep
dreaming of calm seas,
the clear light of Sinera.

Sources

All the poems in this collection are taken from Espriu's nine major published books of poetry, as they appear in the complete edition of his poems, Volume I of his *Obres completes* (1977), published by Edicions 62 in Barcelona.

Sources for the poems in this collection, with the original publication date for each of the volumes from which they come, are as follows:

CEMENTIRI DE SINERA (Cemetery of Sinera) (1946)

What a little nation
I knock at Sinera's
Beside the sea. I had
Hawthorn and holly
Without name or symbol
There will be no marble
When you stop

CANÇONS D'ARIADNA (Songs of Ariadna) (1949)

Grotesque Dance of Death
Small Couplets of the Damned
Flights of Wild Geese
Beginning of Canticle in the Temple
The Wind

LES HORES (The Hours) (1952)

Tree
On Your Death
Offering to Cerberus
Black Land
Winter Journey
Prometheus
Omnis Fortasse Moriar

MRS. DEATH (1952)

Parca
Marriage
The Possessed Man
Stairs
The Garden of Five Trees
Tiresias's Song
Diptych of the Living

EL CAMINANT I EL MUR (The Walker and the Wall) (1954)

Small Echo in the Styx
The Course of Life
From the Theater Itself
Song of Evening's Arrival
Song of Evening's Footsteps
Song of Triumphant Night
Old Brueghel Told It Thus
Book of the Dead
Just Before Lauds
Ish, Isha, Eli, Elis!
Strange Forms, If You Will, Appear in My Mirror
Felt in the Style of Salvador Espriu
Knowles, the Hanged Man, Looks Around from Five Spans Beneath the Branch

FINAL DEL LABERINT (End of the Labyrinth) (1955)

With slow pain the light
I shall speak of the old fire and of water
I have walked the rooms of the house
And then the silence
Bees. The whole swarm
Remember Us
I have left behind the sand and the ship
How the woods surround me!

LA PELL DE BRAU (The Bull's Skin) (1960)

People are many and many are their tongues
The bull, in the arena of Sepharad
They stretch the wings of the sun bird
Don't ask us; better not to know what weariness, what lips
The grape reddens on the vine and suddenly
But you laugh
Our grandparents stared once
Sometimes it is necessary and right

LLIBRE DE SINERA (Book of Sinera) (1963)

Don't you hear the sound the hoe makes
You are in your winter, and this coldness of the earth
Like you today, and like you too, burrowed in tomorrow
This vast, chilling grief
I'll gladly go along, for all the alms
I have come to the naked
But in thirst the pine takes root
Here the voyage ends. When I step off the boat

SETMANA SANTA (Holy Week) (1971)

All they ask is help
Threads of words, unravelings
On what path can light wound you
Eternal, noble, one word